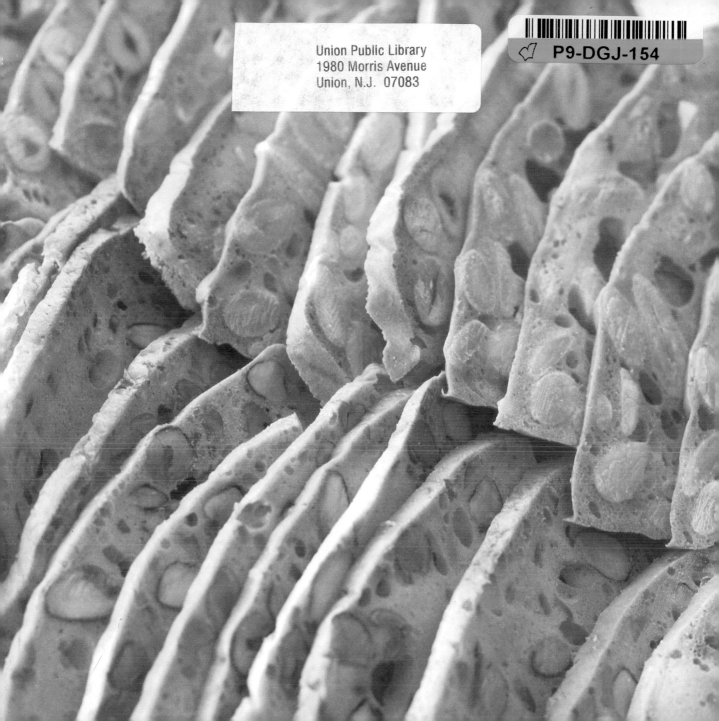
Union Public Library
1980 Morris Avenue
Union, N.J. 07083

P9-DGJ-154

10/08

pâtés &
terrines

pâtés &
terrines

Union Public Library
1980 Morris Avenue
Union, N.J. 07083

Fiona Smith
photography by Peter Cassidy

RYLAND

PETERS

& SMALL

LONDON NEW YORK

First published in the United States
in 2007
by Ryland Peters & Small, Inc.
519 Broadway, 5th Floor
New York, NY 10012
www.rylandpeters.com

10 9 8 7 6 5 4 3 2 1

Text © Fiona Smith 2007
Design and photographs
© Ryland Peters & Small 2007

Printed in China

The author's moral rights have been
asserted. All rights reserved. No part of this
publication may be reproduced, stored in a
retrieval system, or transmitted in any form
or by any means, electronic, mechanical,
photocopying, or otherwise, without the
prior permission of the publisher.

ISBN-10: 1 84597 387 9
ISBN-13: 978 1 84597 387 2

Designers Megan Smith and Liz Sephton
Commissioning Editor Julia Charles
Editor Céline Hughes
Production Gemma Moules
Publishing Director Alison Starling

Food Stylist Linda Tubby
Assistant Food Stylist Rosie Nield
Prop stylist Róisín Nield

Indexer Penelope Kent

Library of Congress Cataloging-in-
Publication Data

Smith, Fiona.
  Pates & terrines / Fiona Smith ;
photography by Peter Cassidy.
    p. cm.
  Includes index.
  ISBN 978-1-84597-387-2
  1. Pâtés (Cookery) 2. Terrines. I. Title. II.
Title: Pates and terrines.
  TX749.S548 2007
  641.8'12--dc22

2006035118

Notes
• All spoon measurements are level unless
otherwise specified.

• All eggs are large unless otherwise
specified. Uncooked or partially cooked eggs
should not be served to the very young, the
frail or elderly, those with compromised
immune systems, or to pregnant women.

• Ovens should be preheated to the
specified temperature. Recipes in this book
were tested in several kinds of oven—all
work slightly differently. I recommend using
an oven thermometer and consulting the
maker's handbook for special instructions.

• All the pâtés and terrines in this book will
keep in the refrigerator for 3 days unless
otherwise stated.

• To clean chicken and duck livers, carefully cut
off any green specks of bile, pull away any
sinew and connective tissue and discard, then
rinse the livers.

contents

introduction

The popularity of terrines and pâtés is deserved. They are both historically important and appealing today; humble yet elegant; suitable for a small bite at a party, a practical appetizer or entrée for the busy cook; and a convenient picnic food.

Terrine is the medieval French word for an ovenproof earthenware cooking dish. It eventually lent its name to the food cooked in it, mostly a rectangular meat, poultry, seafood, or vegetable loaf. The word *pâté* has the same origins, but described a food baked in a pastry case, like a pie. The word then referred to the filling for the pastry, and eventually any reference to pastry was lost, hence "pâté" and "terrine" becoming interchangeable. Pâté evolved into a smoother product and terrine was known for its coarser, sliceable texture.

This book captures the essence of traditional terrines and pâtés, but uses the most modern interpretations: terrine is molded and sliceable; pâté is loose and spreadable. I have also included some rillettes recipes, as they fall between a pâté and a terrine and can be served in the same way.

Traditional terrines used to be very high in fat, but today's palates are less tolerant of highly fatty foods, so in these recipes I have reduced the added fat to a level where the texture is not compromised but the flavor will appeal to contemporary tastes. Lining the terrine with fat (pork back fat or caul) is a traditional step, used to preserve and retain moisture, but in most recipes I have chosen to line the terrine with sliced bacon.

When preparing a terrine, you may like to start by lining the dish first with an opened roasting bag (parchment paper tends to fall apart) or plastic wrap (for nonbaked recipes) to make turning out easier. Alternatively, when the terrine is finished, warm the cold dish in a hot water-bath and run a sharp knife around the edges before turning out.

Placing weights on top of terrines improves the consistency and makes them easier to slice. For cooked terrines, this should be done while still warm. A brick is good for heavy loaf terrines, but you can use cans of food or a loaf pan full of water.

To store meat terrines, wrap them in plastic wrap or parchment paper. Pressing plastic wrap against the cut surface of terrines and pâtés will prevent discoloration due to oxidization. In most cases, terrines and pâtés should be served at room temperature, but I have indicated in individual recipes when this is not the case.

vegetables

This colorful terrine is perfect picnic fare for summer days. Make sure it is kept cold, as it will be difficult to slice at room temperature.

Piquant goat cheese and red bell pepper terrine

6 red bell peppers, halved and seeded

1 tablespoon extra virgin olive oil

8 oz. soft goat cheese

½ cup mascarpone

2 tablespoons freshly squeezed lemon juice

3 tablespoons capers

2 tablespoons snipped fresh dill, plus extra to garnish

¼ teaspoon freshly ground black pepper

slices of crusty bread, and green salad, to serve

a 9-inch loaf pan

Serves 6–8

Put the bell pepper halves, cut-side down, on a baking sheet and place directly under a very hot broiler until blackened. Put the peppers in a bowl, cover with a lid or plastic wrap, and set aside for 10 minutes.

Line the loaf pan with plastic wrap, leaving a generous overhang. Peel off and discard the blackened skin from the peppers. Cut the peppers in half lengthwise and toss with the olive oil. Line the loaf pan with the pepper strips— depending on the height of your pan, they may not come all the way up the sides, which is fine.

In a bowl, mash the goat cheese, mascarpone, and lemon juice to a smooth consistency. Add the capers, dill, and pepper and fold through. Pile the cheese mixture into the lined pan. Fold over the peppers and then the plastic wrap and press down firmly. Refrigerate for at least 4 hours or overnight if you can.

To serve, unfold the plastic wrap and turn the terrine onto a serving plate. Peel off the plastic wrap. Sprinkle the top with a little chopped dill. Slice and serve with crusty bread and a green salad.

The combination of lentil, carrot, and cilantro gives a warming Turkish feel to this spread-like pâté. It is best served with toasted Middle-Eastern bread or Turkish *pide*.

Lentil, carrot, and cilantro pâté

½ cup **Puy lentils**

¼ **cup olive oil**

3 garlic cloves, finely chopped

I onion, chopped

**I teaspoon coriander
seeds, crushed**

**I teaspoon cumin
seeds, crushed**

I teaspoon fresh minced chile

2 large carrots, thickly sliced

⅓ **cup vegetable or
chicken broth**

I tablespoon tomato paste

¼ **cup chopped cilantro, plus
extra leaves to garnish**

**2 tablespoons plain yogurt
(optional)**

extra virgin olive oil, to drizzle

**sea salt and freshly ground
black pepper**

Makes 2½ cups

Rinse the lentils with water, then put them in a saucepan and cover with plenty of water. Bring to a boil, then reduce to a simmer and cook for 15 minutes. Drain and set aside.

Heat the olive oil in a heavy-based saucepan over medium heat. Add the garlic, onion, coriander and cumin seeds, chile, and carrots and cook, stirring, for 5 minutes. Add the cooked lentils, broth, and tomato paste. Reduce to a low simmer, cover, and cook for 15 minutes, stirring occasionally. Leave in the pan, covered, to cool.

Transfer everything to a food processor and process to a thick purée. Season to taste and stir in the cilantro. Put in a serving bowl, stir in the yogurt (if using), and drizzle with a little extra virgin olive oil. Serve garnished with cilantro leaves.

This striking terrine makes an interesting accompaniment to roasted or grilled fish, chicken, or chorizo, or can be served with salad and relish as a vegetarian entrée.

Roast garlic and bean terrine

2 whole garlic heads

¼ cup extra virgin olive oil, plus extra to serve

a small bunch of fresh thyme

two 14-oz. cans cannellini beans, drained and rinsed

3 eggs

½ teaspoon sea salt

¼ teaspoon freshly ground black pepper

16 oz. frozen baby lima beans or 2½ cups shelled fresh butter or baby lima beans

1 onion, chopped

2 tablespoons chopped fresh flatleaf parsley, plus leaves to garnish

a 10-inch loaf pan, oiled and lined with parchment paper

Serves 8

Preheat the oven to 350°F. Cut the tops off the garlic heads, put in a saucepan of boiling water, and boil for 10 minutes. Drain.

Put the garlic heads in a roasting pan, cut-sides up. Sprinkle with 2 tablespoons of the olive oil, then add the thyme and season. Roast for 40 minutes (then leave the oven on for later). Let cool. Squeeze the garlic cloves from the skins and put in a food processor fitted with a metal blade. Add the cannellini beans, 2 of the eggs, and half of the salt and pepper. Process to a smooth purée and set aside.

Cook the lima or butter beans in boiling water for 3 minutes until just tender. Drain and refresh with plenty of cold water.

Sauté the onion in the remaining olive oil for 10 minutes. Put the lima or butter beans, onion with its oil, the remaining egg, salt and pepper, and parsley in the food processor. Process to a smooth purée.

Pour half of the cannellini bean purée into the base of the loaf pan. Spoon over the lima or butter bean purée, then the remaining cannellini bean purée. Put the terrine in a roasting pan and pour enough boiling water into the roasting pan to come halfway up the sides of the terrine.

Bake for 50 minutes, or until the center feels firm. Let cool on a wire rack. Invert onto a plate and remove the paper. Slice and serve drizzled with oil, sprinkled with pepper, and garnished with parsley.

I developed this quick recipe to highlight the wonderful smoky flavors of the smoked mushrooms of Noel Crawford, a New Zealand producer. If you can find presmoked mushrooms, by all means use them—you will need 10 oz. Otherwise, it is quite easy to smoke your own at home.

Smoked mushroom pâté

5 oz. cream cheese

6 anchovies in olive oil, drained, or ½ teaspoon sea salt

6 tablespoons fresh dill

5 tablespoons butter

crackers or toast (page 61), to serve

Smoked mushrooms
½ cup all-purpose flour

½ cup sugar

½ cup rice

¼ cup tea leaves

12 oz. fresh mushrooms

½ cup olive oil

an aluminum foil roasting pan or wok

a large ramekin

Makes 1½ cups

Preheat a grill.

To make the smoked mushrooms, mix together the flour, sugar, rice, and tea and spread over the bottom of the roasting pan or wok.

Put the mushrooms in a single layer on a metal rack. Place the rack on the roasting pan containing the tea-leaf mixture. Cover loosely with a large piece of aluminum foil and crimp the edges securely so that no smoke can escape.

Place on the preheated grill and heat for 15 minutes. Remove from the heat and leave, covered, to cool. Put the cooled mushrooms in a container and cover with the olive oil. Refrigerate until needed.

Put the drained smoked mushrooms, cream cheese, and anchovies in a food processor and process in bursts until well combined. Add 4 tablespoons of the dill and fold through. Spoon the pâté into the ramekin and smooth over the top. Chop the remaining dill and scatter over the pâté.

Melt the butter in a small saucepan. Remove from the heat and let the milk solids settle at the bottom, then pour the clarified butter over the top of the pâté, taking care to pour in as few of the milk solids as possible. Serve with crackers or toast.

If you have mini loaf pans, they are perfect for this terrine. You can use one larger loaf pan, but the terrine will need to be cold to slice easily. This can be served for lunch, before dinner, or even as an interesting cheese course.

Blue cheese, ricotta, and zucchini terrine

2 tablespoons freshly squeezed lemon juice

finely grated peel of 1 unwaxed lemon

½ teaspoon sea salt

3 tablespoons extra virgin olive oil

3 zucchini

6½ oz. soft blue cheese

8 oz. ricotta

6 tablespoons pine nuts, toasted

lemon wedges and slices of seeded bread, to serve

freshly ground black pepper

six 4- x 2¼-inch loaf pans or one 9-inch loaf pan

Serves 6 as lunch, an appetizer, or cheese course

In a glass measuring cup, make the marinade by beating together the lemon juice, peel, salt, and a sprinkling of pepper. Slowly beat in the olive oil.

Slice the zucchini lengthwise as thinly as possible, using a mandoline if you have one. Put in a flat dish and pour over the marinade. Cover and marinate for 1–6 hours, turning occasionally.

Line the loaf pans with plastic wrap, leaving a generous overhang, then use the marinated zucchini strips to line the tins crosswise, leaving enough zucchini overhang to fold over the top when full.

Combine the blue cheese and ricotta. Spoon the mixture into the prepared pans and smooth over the top. Fold over the zucchini and then the plastic wrap and press down firmly. Refrigerate for at least 1 hour to firm up.

To serve, unfold the plastic wrap and turn the terrines onto serving plates. Peel off the plastic wrap. Scatter with the toasted pine nuts and serve with lemon wedges and seeded bread.

Certain vegetables have a rich meatiness that lends them to vegetable pâté—eggplant is one of these. Here, eggplant, olive, and anchovy combine to give a taste of the Mediterranean.

Eggplant, olive, and anchovy pâté

1 large eggplant

2 tablespoons olive oil

2 garlic cloves, crushed

1 onion, very finely chopped

12 anchovy fillets in olive oil, drained and finely chopped

2 tablespoons freshly squeezed lemon juice

¼ cup finely chopped fresh flatleaf parsley

¼ cup torn fresh basil, plus extra leaves to garnish

⅓ cup pitted green or black olives, chopped

slices of white bread, to serve

Makes 1½ cups

Hold the eggplant with tongs directly over the flame of a gas burner or grill, or place it directly under a preheated broiler, turning regularly until blackened and soft. Put in a large bowl, cover with a lid or plastic wrap, and set aside for 10 minutes. Peel off and discard the blackened skin. Cut off the stalk and finely chop the flesh of the eggplant.

Heat the olive oil in a skillet over medium heat and sauté the garlic and onion for 5 minutes until soft. Transfer to a serving dish and combine with the chopped eggplant, anchovies, lemon juice, parsley, basil, and olives. Serve with white bread.

fish & shellfish

This light terrine makes an elegant start to a special-occasion dinner.
Lobster is perfect, but you can replace it with cooked crayfish, shrimp,
langoustines, or scallops.

Lobster and wasabi terrine with radish salad

1 cup light cream
1½ teaspoons powdered gelatin
3 tablespoons hot water
1½–2 teaspoons wasabi
8 oz. cooked lobster meat

Radish salad
6-inch piece of small daikon
  radish, peeled
6 small red radishes, trimmed
1 tablespoon fresh
  cilantro leaves
1 tablespoon Japanese
  soy sauce
1 tablespoon freshly squeezed
  lemon or lime juice
1 tablespoon rice vinegar
1 tablespoon sugar,
  preferably palm

six 4-oz. ramekins, lightly oiled
  with canola

Serves 6

Put the cream in a small saucepan and gently heat until nearly boiling (do not boil). Remove from the heat.

Sprinkle the gelatin over the hot water, let soften for a few minutes, then stir until the gelatin has dissolved. Beat into the cream with the wasabi.

Coarsely chop the lobster meat and divide it between the prepared ramekins. Pour over the wasabi mixture, cover with plastic wrap, and refrigerate for 6 hours or overnight to set.

To make the radish salad, cut the daikon into fine matchsticks using a mandoline, if you have one, and put in a bowl. Cut the red radish into thin slices and add to the bowl with the cilantro.

In a separate bowl, combine the soy sauce, lemon juice, vinegar, and sugar and stir until the sugar has dissolved. Pour the mixture over the radishes and mix. Cover and refrigerate until needed.

When the terrine has set, run a small, sharp knife around the inside of the ramekins, then dip each ramekin into a bowl of freshly boiled water for about 5 seconds, being careful not to get any water in the terrine. Tip each ramekin upside down onto serving plates and tap the base until the terrine slides out. Serve with the radish salad.

A wonderfully quick pâté using smoked mackerel or any other moist smoked fish, this makes a simple yet impressive and delicious start to a dinner party.

Smoked mackerel and preserved lemon pâté
with harissa crushed tomatoes

8 oz. smoked mackerel fillets, skinned

peel of 1 small preserved or fresh lemon, finely chopped

3 tablespoons finely snipped fresh dill

8 oz. cream cheese, softened

10 oz. cherry tomatoes

1 tablespoon harissa (Tunisian hot sauce)

Sumac Crisps (page 55), to serve

6–8 ramekins

Serves 6–8 as an appetizer

Remove any stray bones from the mackerel fillets, flake the mackerel into a bowl, and mix with the lemon peel, dill, and cream cheese. Cover and refrigerate until ready to serve.

In a small serving bowl, combine the cherry tomatoes and harissa, crushing the tomatoes lightly with the back of a fork.

Divide the pâté between the ramekins and serve with Sumac Crisps and the harissa crushed tomatoes.

A mousseline is the traditional base for many delicate terrines and can be made with fish or chicken. The trickiest part of the process is pressing the mixture through a strainer. I like to bake the mousselines in Chinese teacups, but a dariole mold will do.

Shrimp mousseline with asparagus

8 oz. firm white fish fillets, skinned and roughly chopped

1 egg white

¼ teaspoon sea salt

½ cup heavy cream

⅓ cup light cream

5 oz. raw shrimp, shelled, deveined, and finely chopped

2 tablespoons snipped fresh chives

freshly ground black pepper

To serve
cooked asparagus spears
lemon wedges
slices of sourdough bread

six 4-oz. dariole molds or ceramic cups, lightly oiled with a flavorless oil, such as canola

Serves 6

Put the fish fillets in a food processor and process to a smooth purée. While the motor is running, add the egg white and process to combine. Transfer a little of the mixture to a strainer and, using a rubber spatula, press the fish through the strainer into a small bowl, leaving behind any membranes and connective tissue. Discard these, then repeat with the remaining mixture until all the fish has been pressed through the strainer. Press a piece of plastic wrap over the surface of the fish, then put the bowl in a larger bowl half-filled with ice. Chill in the refrigerator for 1 hour.

Preheat the oven to 300°F.

Using a wooden spoon, stir the salt into the fish mixture, then gradually beat in the heavy and light creams. Finally, stir in the shrimp and chives.

Spoon the mixture into the prepared molds or cups and smooth over the tops. Put the dishes in a roasting pan, then pour in enough water to come halfway up the sides of the dishes. Bake in the oven for 35–40 minutes until firm. Let cool slightly, then turn out onto serving plates if you used molds, or serve still in the cups. Sprinkle with pepper and serve with a few asparagus spears, some lemon wedges, and slices of sourdough bread.

Pressed, uncooked terrines are popular for their simplicity and clean flavors. You can use almost any seafood here, but I like the color and richness of salmon in contrast with the leeks. The terrine must be weighted down so the ingredients press together and become sliceable.

Pressed salmon and leek terrine with mustard sauce

2 cups good-quality fish broth

1¾ lb. salmon fillets

3 lb. baby leeks, washed and trimmed

fresh chives, to garnish

sea salt and freshly ground black pepper

Mustard sauce

¼ cup freshly squeezed lemon juice

6 tablespoons crème fraîche or sour cream

2 tablespoons Dijon mustard

2 teaspoons honey

3 tablespoons snipped fresh chives (optional)

a 10-inch loaf pan

Serves 10–12 as a light summer lunch or appetizer

Line the loaf pan with a double thickness of plastic wrap, leaving a large overhang on both sides. To make the mustard sauce, beat together all the ingredients in a bowl and season to taste. Set aside.

Put the broth and salmon fillets in a large saucepan. Cover, bring to a gentle simmer, and continue cooking for 2–4 minutes, depending on the thickness of the salmon. Do not boil. Remove the pan from the heat and let cool for 15 minutes. Remove the salmon, peel off the skin, and discard it. Break the salmon into large pieces.

Put the leeks in a large steamer over boiling water, cover, and steam for 15 minutes until tender. Quickly refresh with cold water.

Season both the leeks and the salmon to taste. Put a third of the leeks in the bottom of the loaf pan, parallel to the long sides, then layer half of the salmon pieces over the top. Repeat this process, finishing with a final layer of leeks. Fold the plastic wrap over the top. Slash the top and around the sides in several places with the point of a sharp knife to allow any excess juices to escape. Put the terrine on a tray and weight the top down well (page 6). Refrigerate overnight.

Unfold the plastic wrap from the terrine, invert onto a serving dish, and peel off the plastic wrap. Slice with a sharp knife into ¾-inch slices. Serve with the mustard sauce and garnished with a few chives.

A treat for lovers of smoked salmon, this rich terrine is best accompanied with the creamy, bitter tastes of the avocado and pink grapefruit salad. You could also serve it for breakfast with cream cheese, bagels, and lemon wedges.

Individual smoked salmon terrines
with avocado and pink grapefruit salad

10 oz. smoked salmon, cut into wide strips

10-oz. piece hot-smoked salmon

freshly squeezed juice of I lemon

3 tablespoons snipped fresh dill, plus sprigs to garnish

trout or salmon roe, to garnish

Avocado and pink grapefruit salad

3 thick slices white bread

3 tablespoons avocado oil or light olive oil

I pink grapefruit

I large avocado

six 4-oz. dariole molds

Serves 6 as an appetizer or lunch

Line the dariole molds with plastic wrap, leaving a generous overhang. Line the molds with the strips of smoked salmon, leaving enough salmon overhang to fold over the top when filled.

In a bowl, mash together the hot-smoked salmon, lemon juice, and dill. Spoon this mixture into the prepared molds and smooth over the top. Fold over the salmon and then the plastic wrap, and press down firmly. Refrigerate for at least I hour to firm up.

To make the avocado and pink grapefruit salad, slice the crusts off the bread and discard. Cut the bread into ½ inch cubes. Heat 2 tablespoons of the avocado oil in a skillet and sauté the bread until you get golden croutons. Set aside.

Slice the top and bottom from the grapefruit and remove the peel and any pith. Carefully slice between each segment and remove the flesh. Put the segments in a bowl.

Peel the avocado, remove the pit, and cut the flesh into ½-inch cubes. Toss with the grapefruit, croutons, and the remaining oil.

To serve the terrines, unfold the plastic wrap and turn onto serving plates. Peel off the plastic wrap. Garnish with trout roe and dill sprigs, and serve with the avocado and pink grapefruit salad.

This delicate pâté relies on getting as much flavor as possible out of slow-cooked onions, and the quality of a few simple ingredients. It is best to use tuna preserved in olive oil, in a jar, but you may use canned tuna.

Tuna and caramelized onion pâté

3 tablespoons olive oil

3 large onions, thinly sliced

1 tablespoon finely chopped fresh flatleaf parsley

6½-oz. jar tuna in olive oil

sea salt and freshly ground black pepper

toast (page 61), to serve

Makes 1½ cups

Heat the olive oil in a large, heavy-based saucepan over very low heat. Add the onions and cook gently for 1 hour, stirring occasionally, until the onions are very soft and just turning golden. Remove from the heat.

Mix together the onions, parsley, and tuna, with its preserving oil, and season to taste. For a smoother pâté, process the ingredients in a food processor. Transfer to a serving dish and serve with toast.

poultry

There are many variations on the classic chicken liver pâté: try one of the flavoring suggestions below. If you like a creamy pâté, use cream; for a rich, delicate pâté, use butter; and for a strong pâté, use soy sauce.

Chicken liver pâté

3 tablespoons butter

I onion, finely chopped

2 garlic cloves, chopped

2 bay leaves

I lb. chicken livers, cleaned and trimmed (page 4)

2 tablespoons Cognac (optional)

I teaspoon Worcestershire sauce

½ teaspoon sea salt

¼ teaspoon freshly ground black pepper

¼ teaspoon ground nutmeg

½ cup cream, 6½ tablespoons softened butter, or 2 tablespoons soy sauce

flavoring of choice (optional)*

butter, duck or goose fat, or powdered gelatin and chicken broth, to seal

caperberries and Melba Toast (page 61), to serve

Makes 2 cups

Heat the butter in a large skillet over medium heat and sauté the onion, garlic, and bay leaves for 5 minutes. Increase the heat, add the chicken livers, and cook, stirring constantly, for 2–3 minutes until firm but still pink in the middle. Add the Cognac (if using) and flambé. Remove from the heat and discard the bay leaves.

Put the mixture in a food processor fitted with a metal blade and add the Worcestershire sauce, salt, pepper, nutmeg, cream, and flavoring of choice (if using). Process in short bursts until you have a smooth pâté. Pile into ramekins, smooth the top over, and finish with one of the toppings below. Serve with caperberries and Melba Toast.

To seal with butter or fat, melt 5 tablespoons butter, duck, or goose fat and pour over the top of the pâté. To seal with aspic, dissolve I teaspoon powdered gelatin in ⅔ cup hot chicken broth. Cool slightly and pour over the pâté. Garnish as desired. Store the pâté in the refrigerator for up to I week if fully sealed, or 3 days if not.

* To flavor with cracked pepper, increase the quantity of pepper to ½ teaspoon and scatter the finished pâté with 2 tablespoons lightly crushed colored peppercorns.

To flavor with herbs, add ¼ cup chopped fresh chervil, parsley, or tarragon to the mixture in the food processor. Garnish the top of the pâté with a few whole sprigs of the same herb.

Chicken liver pâté with blueberry and balsamic glaze

2 tablespoons olive oil

1 onion, finely chopped

2 garlic cloves, chopped

2 bay leaves

1 lb. chicken livers, cleaned and trimmed (page 4)

1 tablespoon balsamic cream or port

2 teaspoons soy sauce

¼ teaspoon ground nutmeg

¼ teaspoon ground cinnamon

½ teaspoon sea salt

¼ teaspoon freshly ground black pepper

fresh thyme, to garnish (optional)

grissini (Italian bread sticks), to serve

Blueberry and balsamic glaze
1¼ cups fresh or frozen blueberries

3 tablespoons sugar

1½ teaspoons powdered gelatin

1 tablespoon balsamic vinegar

6 ramekins or small glass dishes

Serves 6

This is a less rich, dairy-free alternative to traditional chicken liver pâté, with an attractive fruity glaze. If you can't find balsamic cream, you can boil balsamic vinegar until reduced by half. This pâté will keep for 1 week if sealed with fat or gelatin, or up to 3 days if not.

To make the blueberry and balsamic glaze, put the blueberries, sugar, and ⅓ cup water in a saucepan. Bring to a boil, then continue to cook for 3 minutes. Strain through a fine strainer to give about ⅔ cup.

Sprinkle the powdered gelatin over the hot blueberry mixture and let soften for a few minutes. Add the balsamic vinegar and stir until the gelatin has dissolved. Let cool slightly before using.

Heat the olive oil in a large skillet over medium heat and sauté the onion, garlic, and bay leaves for 5 minutes until translucent but not yet brown. Increase the heat, add the chicken livers, and cook, stirring constantly, for 2–3 minutes until firm but still pink in the middle. Remove from the heat and discard the bay leaves.

Put the chicken liver mixture in a food processor fitted with a metal blade and add the balsamic cream, soy sauce, nutmeg, cinnamon, salt, and pepper. Process in short bursts until you have a smooth pâté.

Pile the pâté into the ramekins, smooth the tops, and pour over the blueberry and balsamic glaze. Garnish with thyme (if using) and serve with grissini. Store in the refrigerator for up to 1 week.

Chicken, carrot, and tarragon terrine

I large, whole chicken

I onion, sliced

4 whole garlic cloves, peeled

2 tablespoons sliced
   fresh ginger

½ teaspoon freshly ground
   black pepper

I teaspoon sea salt

4 large carrots, peeled

1½ cups flavorful chicken broth

I tablespoon powdered gelatin

½ cup fresh tarragon leaves

½ cup slivered almonds, toasted

lettuce leaves, to serve

a 10-inch loaf pan or
*   terrine mold*

Serves 6–8 as lunch
**   or light dinner**

This is a much lighter version of a classic terrine, and although it is set with a gelatinous stock, it bears no resemblance to those aspic-covered terrines of the '70s.

Preheat the oven to 350°F.

Put the chicken, breast-side down, in a roasting pan and stuff with the onion, garlic, and ginger. Rub all over with the pepper and salt. Put the carrots around the chicken and pour over I cup of the broth. Roast in the oven for 80 minutes, turning the carrots once. Remove from the oven, cover with aluminum foil, and let cool.

Pour the broth and any juices off the chicken into a glass measuring cup and make up to 1½ cups with the remaining broth. Bring to boiling point. Sprinkle the powdered gelatin into the broth stock, let soften for a few minutes, and stir to dissolve.

Remove the skin from the chicken, slice the meat from the bones, then finely shred. Slice the carrots diagonally into ⅛-inch slices.

Line the loaf pan with plastic wrap, leaving enough overhang to cover the finished terrine. Arrange a third of the tarragon on the bottom, followed by a third of the chicken, a third of the tarragon and half of the carrots, then pour over a third of the broth. Cover with another layer of chicken, tarragon, carrots, and broth. Finish with the remaining chicken and broth. Bang the terrine to settle the ingredients. Cover with the plastic wrap, put a weight on top, and refrigerate overnight until set. Unwrap the terrine, invert onto a serving plate, and remove the plastic wrap. Scatter with the almonds and serve with lettuce.

Jewish-style chopped liver with egg makes a simple, loose pâté. Use the best-quality free-range livers, as they are a key flavor in the dish. The pâté is perfect served with zhoug, a traditional Jewish fresh herb salsa.

Chopped liver with zhoug

¼ cup olive oil, plus extra
   to serve
1 onion, chopped
1 lb. chicken livers, cleaned and
   trimmed (page 4)
4 eggs
sea salt and freshly ground
   black pepper
sweet paprika and matzo
   crackers, to serve

Zhoug
1 teaspoon cumin seeds
4 large mild green chiles,
   seeded and chopped
½ cup fresh flatleaf parsley
½ cup cilantro
1 garlic clove, chopped
½ cup olive oil

**Serves 4–6 as lunch or
   10 as a snack**

To make the zhoug, heat a small skillet and toast the cumin seeds for 30 seconds until just fragrant. Remove from the heat and crush with a mortar and pestle. Put in a small food processor or large mortar and pestle with the chiles, parsley, cilantro, and garlic and blend to a rough paste, adding the olive oil slowly as you do so. Season. Store in an airtight container in the refrigerator for up to 2 weeks.

Heat 2 tablespoons of the olive oil in a large skillet over medium heat and sauté the onion for 6 minutes, or until soft and pale golden. Set aside.

Season the livers. Heat another tablespoon of the oil over high heat and cook half of the livers for 2 minutes (for rare) or 4 minutes (for medium). Set aside and cook the remaining livers.

Fill a saucepan with water, add the eggs, and put over medium/high heat. Bring to a boil and cook for 4–6 minutes until the eggs are hard-cooked. Drain and refresh with cold water. Let cool, then peel.

Finely chop the livers and eggs and combine in a bowl with the onion. Season to taste. Transfer to a serving dish, drizzle with olive oil, and sprinkle with a little paprika. Serve with the zhoug and matzo crackers.

Turkey, caper, and chile pâté

¾ cup prepared gravy
  or freshly made gravy
  (see below)

2 tablespoons mayonnaise

4 scallions, chopped

2 large mild red chiles,
  seeded and chopped

2 tablespoons capers

crackers, to serve

Poached turkey

1 lb. turkey breast, skin on

1 small onion, sliced

a small bunch of fresh parsley

1 celery stalk, chopped

1½ cups flavorful chicken broth

Gravy

3 tablespoons olive oil

3 tablespoons flour

1 cup chicken broth

sea salt and freshly ground
  black pepper

Makes 2½ cups

I developed this creamy yet dairy-free pâté over Christmas as a great way of using up leftover turkey or chicken meat and gravy. Use 9 oz. ready-cooked turkey, or make the pâté from scratch by poaching uncooked turkey. If you are making your own gravy, use the broth from the poached turkey, as it will be full of flavor.

To make the poached turkey, put the turkey breast, onion, parsley, and celery in a saucepan and cover with the broth. Bring to a simmer and continue to cook, partially covered, for 15–20 minutes, depending on the thickness of the turkey breast. Turn off the heat, cover, and let the turkey cool in the broth for 20 minutes. Discard the skin.

To make fresh gravy, heat the olive oil in a saucepan over medium heat and stir in the flour. Cook, stirring constantly, for 2 minutes, then slowly stir in the broth. Cook, stirring constantly, for a further 2–3 minutes until thick. Season well.

Put the turkey meat in a food processor with the gravy, mayonnaise, scallions, and chiles and process in bursts until you have a coarse pâté. Stir in the capers and transfer to a serving dish. Serve with crackers.

meat & game

I love the simplicity of this chunky pork terrine, flavored with fennel seeds and layered with spinach. Its small size makes it perfect for a small party of guests or to serve for a simple snack or lunch.

Pork, fennel, and spinach terrine with drunken figs

2 bay leaves

5 oz. sliced bacon

2 cups spinach, chopped

2 tablespoons olive oil

1 small onion, chopped

1 tablespoon fennel seeds

2 garlic cloves, finely chopped

10 oz. ground pork

7 oz. pork tenderloin, diced

½ teaspoon ground nutmeg

½ teaspoon ground allspice

1 teaspoon sea salt

½ teaspoon black pepper

slices of crusty bread, to serve

Drunken figs

20 dried Turkish figs, halved

1 cup Marsala wine

a small terrine mold or loaf pan, oiled with canola oil

Serves 6

To make the drunken figs, put the figs, Marsala, and ¼ cup water in a saucepan and bring nearly to boiling point. Remove from the heat, cover, and let cool. Store in an airtight container in the refrigerator for up to 2 weeks.

Preheat the oven to 350°F. Arrange the bay leaves over the bottom of the terrine mold, then lay the bacon across the width. Put the spinach in a colander and pour over boiling water to blanch. Refresh with cold water, squeeze out any excess water, and set aside.

Heat the olive oil in a skillet over low heat and sauté the onion, fennel seeds, and garlic for 10 minutes, or until soft but not yet brown. Transfer to a large bowl with half of the spinach, all the pork, the nutmeg, and allspice. Add the salt and pepper and mix well.

Put half of the pork mixture in the prepared terrine mold and press down firmly. Top with the spinach, then the remaining pork mixture. Press down firmly, then fold over any overhanging bacon. Firmly cover with oiled aluminum foil and put in a baking dish. Fill the baking dish with enough water to come halfway up the sides of the terrine. Bake in the oven for 1 hour. Transfer to a dish to catch any juices and put a weight on top (page 6). Let cool, then chill overnight or for 1–2 days. Serve with the drunken figs and crusty bread.

A parfait or mousse is the smoothest, most delicate way of preparing livers, and perfect for the velvety richness of duck. You can replace the duck livers with chicken if you like a very smooth chicken liver pâté.

Duck liver mousse with pistachio wafers

2 tablespoons unsalted butter, plus 4 tablespoons, softened

1 shallot, very finely chopped

1 lb. duck livers, cleaned and trimmed (page 4)

3 tablespoons Cognac, port, Madeira wine, or sherry (optional)

¼ teaspoon sea salt

⅛ teaspoon ground white pepper

⅓ cup heavy cream

To serve
pistachio wafers (page 60)
Spiced Pickled Cherries (page 62)

Makes 2 cups

Melt 1 tablespoon of the butter in a skillet over low heat and sauté the shallot for 5 minutes, or until very soft but not yet brown. Put in a food processor fitted with a metal blade.

Melt the remaining tablespoon of butter in the same skillet over high heat, add the duck livers, and sauté for 2–3 minutes until just seared. Add the Cognac (if using) and flambé.

Put the livers in the food processor with the shallot and process in short bursts until finely puréed. Tip the mixture into a strainer and, using the back of a wooden spoon, press the mixture through into a bowl. Scrape any residue from the bottom of the strainer into the bowl. Mix in the softened butter, salt, and pepper. Let cool.

Whip the cream to soft peaks, then fold into the liver mixture.

Spoon the mousse into a dish, smooth over the top, and press a piece of plastic wrap over the top to prevent discoloration. Refrigerate until needed.

Spoon the mousse out in sausage shapes onto small plates and serve with pistachio wafers and Spiced Pickled Cherries. Alternatively, it can be spooned into tiny tart cases as hors d'oeuvre.

Duck terrine with citrus salad

12 oz. pork fat, sliced ¾ inch thick

5 duck breasts, about 8 oz. each

3 tablespoons olive oil

6½ oz. sliced bacon

1 small onion, finely chopped

1 bay leaf

½ teaspoon ground allspice

½ teaspoon ground nutmeg

1 lb. duck or chicken livers, cleaned and trimmed (page 4)

8 oz. ground pork

¾ cup fresh bread crumbs

1 egg, beaten

finely grated peel of 2 oranges

2 tablespoons fresh thyme leaves

1 teaspoon sea salt

½ cup orange juice

¼ cup Grand Marnier or brandy

¼ teaspoon saltpeter, available at pharmacies and butchers (optional)

Citrus salad
3 limes and 3 oranges

4 cups watercress

extra virgin olive oil

a 3-quart terrine mold

Serves 10–12

Preheat the oven to 325°F. Line the sides and base of the terrine mold with the pork fat, reserving enough for the top.

Remove the skin and fat from the duck breasts and discard. Slice 3 of the duck breasts into pieces and put in a food processor. Heat a skillet until very hot. Rub the remaining duck breasts with a little olive oil and sear on both sides. Remove from the skillet and wrap with the bacon. Set aside. Reduce the heat and add the remaining olive oil. Sauté the onion, bay leaf, allspice, and nutmeg for 5 minutes. Discard the bay leaf, put the rest in the food processor with the duck, and process until coarsely chopped. Put in a large bowl and set aside.

Put the duck livers in the food processor and process to a smooth purée. Add to the bowl along with the ground pork, bread crumbs, egg, orange peel, thyme leaves, and salt. In a glass measuring cup, combine the orange juice, Grand Marnier, and saltpeter (if using) and stir to dissolve. Add to the mixture and mix well.

Put half of the mixture in the terrine and press flat. Lay the whole duck breasts over the top, then cover with the remaining mixture. Smooth over the top and cover with the reserved fat. Firmly cover with oiled aluminum foil and put in a baking dish. Pour enough water in the dish to come halfway up the terrine. Bake for 75 minutes.

Remove the terrine from the oven, put in a dish to catch any juices, and put a weight on top (page 6). Let cool, then refrigerate overnight or for 1–2 days. To make the citrus salad, slice the top and bottom from the fruit and cut off the peel and any pith. Carefully slice between each segment and remove the flesh. Combine with the watercress and a little extra virgin olive oil, and serve with a slice of terrine.

A traditional means of preserving meat in fat, rillettes are a delicious and simple alternative to a heartier terrine. The absence of liver makes it appealing to those who do not like it.

Pork and hazelnut rillettes with pickled cucumbers

2¼ lb. very fatty pork butt

7 fresh thyme sprigs

2 whole, large garlic cloves, peeled

1 bay leaf

1 teaspoon sea salt

½ teaspoon freshly ground black pepper

½ cup white wine

½ cup hazelnuts

Pickled cucumbers
6-inch length of cucumber

½ cup rice vinegar

½ cup sugar

six 4-oz. pots or one 3-cup pot

Makes 2½ cups

To make the pickled cucumbers, cut the cucumber in half lengthwise and scoop out the seeds. Cut the flesh into very thin strips.

Put the rice vinegar and sugar in a saucepan and bring to a boil, stirring until the sugar has dissolved. Boil for 3 minutes. Cool and pour over the cucumber. Cover and refrigerate until needed.

Cut the pork butt into small pieces and put in a small, heavy-based casserole dish. Add 1 thyme sprig (reserving the rest as a garnish), the garlic, bay leaf, salt, and pepper and pour over the wine. Cover and cook over low heat for 3 hours until the meat is very tender.

Preheat the oven to 325°F.

While the pork is cooking, spread the hazelnuts in an even layer over a baking sheet. Bake in the oven for 20 minutes, stirring occasionally, until the nuts are just smelling toasted. Put them in a clean kitchen towel and rub vigorously until the skins come loose. Discard the skins and roughly chop the nuts.

Pour the pork into a colander over a bowl or pitcher, reserving all the juices. Using 2 forks, tear the pork into fine strips, or process briefly in a food processor. Combine the meat with the toasted hazelnuts and pack into the pots. Spoon the fatty juices over the meat and finish with a thyme sprig to garnish.

These little potted meats are somewhere between a pâté and a terrine. As they are not cooked, you can set them in any little dishes you fancy. Whole green peppercorns add a real kick, but if you like a mild flavor, use mustard.

Ham and chicken pots with cornichons

10 oz. chicken breasts, skin on

1 onion, thickly sliced

½ teaspoon black peppercorns

½ teaspoon sea salt

2 cups chicken broth

1 tablespoon powdered gelatin

¼ cup verjuice or dry white wine

10 oz. thickly sliced ham

¼ cup chopped fresh flatleaf parsley

1 tablespoon green peppercorns in brine, drained, or whole-grain mustard

slices of crusty bread, and cornichons (gherkins), to serve

6 ramekins

Serves 6

Put the chicken breasts in a saucepan with the onion, black peppercorns, and salt. Add the chicken broth. Heat to boiling point, then reduce to a low simmer. Cook, partially covered, for 15–20 minutes, depending on the thickness of the chicken breasts. Remove from the heat, cover tightly, and leave off the heat to continue cooking for a further 20 minutes. Remove the breasts from the broth (reserving the broth), let cool, and discard the skin, then cut the meat into small dice.

Drain 1¼ cups of the hot broth into a pitcher. Put the powdered gelatin in the hot broth, let soften for a few minutes, then stir to dissolve. Stir in the verjuice.

Put the ham in a food processor fitted with a metal blade and process in bursts until finely chopped.

In a bowl, combine the chicken, ham, parsley, and green peppercorns. Divide the mixture between the ramekins. Pour over the gelatinous broth. Refrigerate for 3–4 hours until set. Serve with crusty bread and cornichons.

This pâté is real party fare. It was inspired by "tinga," Mexican shredded beef, and relies on slow cooking and a few key flavors.

Beef and ale pâté

¾ cup dried pinto beans

2 tablespoons olive oil

5 large, mild red chiles

3 whole garlic cloves, peeled

I large, dried mulatto or ancho chile (optional)

1¼ lb. blade steak, trimmed of fat and cut into 1-inch chunks

two 12-oz. bottles of ale

sea salt

½ cup cilantro leaves, to garnish

tortilla chips or crusty rolls, to serve

Makes 3 cups

Soak the beans in cold water overnight. Drain, put in a saucepan, and cover with plenty of water. Bring to a boil and continue to boil for 10 minutes. Drain the beans and set aside.

Heat the olive oil in a large, heavy-based saucepan over medium/low heat. Cut the green stalk ends from 3 of the red chiles. Put these chiles and the garlic in the saucepan and gently cook for 3 minutes. If using, cut the dried chile in half and remove the seeds and stalk. Add the flesh to the saucepan and continue cooking for 2 minutes. Increase the heat to medium/high, add the steak and cook, stirring occasionally, for 5 minutes until the meat is brown.

Add the ale and beans to the saucepan and bring to a boil. Reduce the heat to a slow simmer, cover, and cook for 1½ hours, stirring occasionally.

Uncover the saucepan and cook for 1 hour until the meat is falling apart. Put the meat with its accompanying ingredients and a little of the cooking liquid in a food processor and process briefly until you have a coarse pâté. Season with salt to taste.

Spoon into a serving dish. Cut the remaining red chiles into thin strips and scatter over the pâté with the cilantro. Serve warm or at room temperature with tortilla chips or crusty rolls.

This spicy, slow-cooked duck gives a modern twist to the classic rillettes, and the sumac crisps make an unusual accompaniment.

Spiced duck rillettes with sumac crisps

4 duck leg and thigh pieces

1 teaspoon sea salt

2 garlic cloves

**3 tablespoons finely sliced
  fresh ginger**

**1 cinnamon stick, crushed,
  plus 6 more to garnish**

6 whole cloves

**2 teaspoons crushed
  allspice berries**

2 teaspoons cumin seeds

**½ teaspoon dried red
  pepper flakes**

**Spiced Pickled Cherries
  (page 62), to serve**

Sumac crisps

3 pita breads

2 tablespoons olive oil

1 tablespoon ground sumac

**2 tablespoons fresh
  thyme leaves**

six 4-oz. pots or one 3-cup pot

Serves 6

Preheat the oven to 350°F.

To make the sumac crisps, split the pita breads in half and put on a baking sheet, rough-sides up. Brush with the olive oil and sprinkle the sumac and thyme leaves over the top. Bake in the oven for 15 minutes until golden. Let cool on a rack. Break the cooled bread into cracker-size pieces. The sumac crisps can be stored in an airtight container for up to 1 week.

Reduce the oven to 325°F.

Put the duck pieces in small, heavy-based casserole dish and rub with the salt. Add the garlic, ginger, cinnamon stick, cloves, allspice, cumin seeds, and pepper flakes, and pour over ½ cup water. Cover and cook in the oven for 2 hours until the meat is very tender. Remove the duck from the casserole dish (reserving the juices), pull off the skin, and discard it. Using 2 forks, tear the meat from the bones and discard the bones. Shred the meat into fine strips.

Pack the duck into the pots. Spoon the duck juices over the meat, taking care not to include too many of the whole spices. Scatter the top with a few of the large spices and the extra cinnamon sticks to garnish. Serve with the sumac crisps and Spiced Pickled Cherries.

Farmhouse terrine

7 oz. sliced bacon

3 tablespoons olive oil

8 oz. chicken livers, cleaned and trimmed (page 4)

1 small onion, chopped

2 garlic cloves, finely chopped

2 lb. very fatty pork butt, coarsely ground

8 oz. veal or chicken, ground

½ cup fresh bread crumbs

½ cup chopped fresh parsley

1 tablespoon chopped fresh thyme

1 tablespoon chopped fresh oregano

½ teaspoon ground nutmeg

½ teaspoon ground allspice

1 teaspoon sea salt

½ teaspoon black pepper

¼ cup brandy

½ cup chicken broth

6 bay or sage leaves

radishes and slices of crusty bread, to serve

a 5-cup terrine mold or loaf pan, oiled with canola oil

Serves 10–12

Every home needs a pâté maison, a classic, rustic farmhouse terrine, full of your favorite flavors. Traditionally, it would have included lard to give a much softer loaf, but this is my version—healthier, lighter, and packed with flavor.

Preheat the oven to 350°F. Lay some of the bacon across the width of the prepared terrine, reserving some for the top.

Heat 1 tablespoon of the olive oil in a skillet over high heat and cook the chicken livers for 1 minute until just colored. Remove from the skillet, coarsely chop, and set aside. Reduce the heat to low and add the remaining oil. Sauté the onion and garlic for 10 minutes until soft but not yet brown. Put the onion, garlic, livers, and all the remaining ingredients, except the bay leaves, in a large bowl and mix until well combined.

Pack the mixture into the terrine and press down firmly. Fold over any overhanging bacon, cover with the reserved bacon, and finish with the bay leaves. Cover firmly with the terrine lid or a sheet of oiled aluminum foil and place in a baking dish. Fill the baking dish with enough water to come halfway up the sides of the terrine. Bake in the oven for 75 minutes.

Remove the terrine from the oven and put it in a dish to catch any juices. Put a weight over the top (page 6) and let cool. Refrigerate overnight or for 1–2 days. Serve with radishes and crusty bread.

Prosciutto and pumpkin terrine with celeriac salad

5 oz. thinly sliced prosciutto

1¾ lb. pie pumpkin or
   butternut squash

2 tablespoons olive oil

2 tablespoons fresh thyme
   leaves, plus sprigs to garnish

3 eggs

1 tablespoon pure maple syrup

¼ teaspoon ground nutmeg

½ teaspoon sea salt

¼ teaspoon freshly ground
   black pepper

Celeriac salad

1 celeriac

3 tablespoons chopped fresh
   flatleaf parsley

2 tablespoons good-quality
   mayonnaise

1 tablespoon freshly squeezed
   lemon juice

1 tablespoon olive oil

sea salt and freshly ground
   black pepper

a 10-inch terrine mold,
   lightly oiled

Serves 8–10

This light, savory terrine is fantastic for summer lunches and light suppers, and perfect for returning home to after a night out. It is best served just warm or at room temperature—if it is too hot, it will be hard to slice. Always try to cut between the prosciutto slices.

Preheat the oven to 350°F.

Cut the prosciutto into 1-inch strips and lay them across the width of the prepared terrine mold.

Cut the skin off the pumpkin and discard it. Cut the flesh into 1-inch cubes and toss with the olive oil and the thyme leaves. Spread in a roasting pan and roast in the oven for 30 minutes until soft.

Let the pumpkin cool slightly, then put in a food processor and process to a purée. Add the eggs, maple syrup, nutmeg, salt, and pepper and process until well mixed. Pour the mixture into the terrine mold and bake in the oven for 30 minutes. Cover the terrine with a sheet of oiled aluminum foil and bake for a further 15 minutes until the pumpkin is set. Remove from the oven and let cool for at least 15 minutes before serving. Turn the terrine out, then invert so that the prosciutto is around the sides and base.

To make the celeriac salad, finely grate the celeriac into a bowl using a mandoline or grater. Toss with the remaining ingredients. Serve the terrine warm or at room temperature, garnished with thyme sprigs, with the celeriac salad.

accompaniments

I often whip up a batch of these thin, biscuit-like wafers to serve with pâtés, as they look and taste much better than store-bought crackers. Use any nuts you like to complement the flavors in the pâté.

Nut wafers

Preheat the oven to 325°F.

In a bowl, beat the eggs and sugar until well mixed. Fold in the flour and nuts, taking care not to overmix. Spread the mixture into the prepared loaf pan. Bake in the oven for 45 minutes until lightly colored. Let cool on a wire rack.

Wrap the loaf in aluminum foil and refrigerate overnight.

The next day, preheat the oven to 325°F.

Cut the bread diagonally as thinly as you can, using a sharp knife, and lay the slices out on the prepared baking sheets. Bake in the oven for 20–25 minutes until brown. Keep an eye on them in the last 5 minutes of cooking, as they burn easily. Let cool on a wire rack. Store in an airtight container for up to 1 week.

3 eggs

¼ cup sugar

1 cup plus 1½ tablespoons flour

**¾ cup roasted nuts,
(e.g. almond, hazelnut)
skinned where necessary**

*a loaf pan (approx. 8 x 4 inches),
lined with parchment paper*
*2 baking sheets, lined with
parchment paper*

Makes 30 pieces

Melba toast

Melba toast goes especially well with fine, delicate pâtés, such as smooth chicken liver, mousses, and fish terrines.

6 slices medium-slice white bread

Makes 24 toasts

Preheat the broiler to medium.
    Broil the bread on each side until evenly golden. Remove from the heat. Cut the crusts off and discard them, then cut the slices in half horizontally. Cut the toast diagonally in half.
    Put the toasts, uncooked-side up, under the broiler and toast until golden.
    Let cool on a rack and store in an airtight container for up to 1 week.

Crostini

Sturdy crostini suit hearty pâtés, such as lentil pâté, farmhouse terrine, and duck terrine.

1 thin baguette
olive oil

Preheat the oven to 350°F.
    Slice the baguette into ⅜-inch slices and lay on a baking sheet. Brush liberally with olive oil.
    Bake in the oven for 15 minutes, turning once and brushing with more oil.
    Let cool on a rack and store in an airtight container for up to 1 week.

Other breads

Any bread can be toasted or baked for serving with pâtés and terrines.

Preheat the oven to 350°F.
    Put thin slices of any bread (cut to preferred shape) on a baking sheet and spread with butter or brush with olive oil.
    Bake in the oven for 10–15 minutes until golden.
    Let cool on a rack and store in an airtight container for up to 1 week.

Pickled cherries have long been a favorite match for French charcuterie, going especially well with pork and duck. You can use sweet or sour cherries, leaving the stems on for an elegant finish.

Spiced pickled cherries

2¼ cups sugar

2 cups white wine vinegar

2 teaspoons black peppercorns

6 cloves

2 star anise

1 cinnamon stick

**2 lb. sweet or sour fresh
cherries, rinsed**

a large, sterilized jar

Makes about 4 cups

Put the sugar, vinegar, peppercorns, cloves, star anise, and cinnamon in a saucepan and heat, stirring until the sugar has dissolved. Reduce the heat to a simmer and cook for 8 minutes. Let cool.

Sort through the cherries, discarding any that are bruised or split. Pack them into the sterilized jar and pour over the cold liquid with its spices. Seal and store for a few weeks before eating. The cherries will keep for up to a year.

Pickled onions and gherkins are traditional accompaniments to pâtés and terrines, helping to cut through the richness and, in some cases, the fattiness of the dish.

Sweet and sour pickled onions

2 lb. pickling onions (if not in season, use shallots)

2 tablespoons sea salt

1 cinnamon stick

3 small hot red chiles

2 teaspoons black peppercorns

⅓ cup raisins

1 cup sugar

1½ cups white wine vinegar

½ cup Moscatel or sherry vinegar

a large, sterilized jar

Makes about 4 cups

Trim the tops and bottoms off the onions, keeping enough flesh to hold the onions together. Bring a saucepan of water to a boil and remove from the heat. Put the onions in the water and let them sit for 1 minute, then drain.

Have a bowl of ice water ready. Peel the skins off the onions, discard, and drop the onions straight into the ice water. When they are all peeled, drain them and put them in a bowl. Sprinkle them with the salt to coat. Cover with a kitchen towel and leave overnight.

The next day, rinse the onions, dry them on paper towels, and transfer to the sterilized jar.

Put the cinnamon, chiles, peppercorns, raisins, sugar, vinegar, and Moscatel in a saucepan and bring to a boil, stirring until the sugar has dissolved. Pour the hot liquid with its spices over the onions. Seal and store for at least 2 weeks before serving. Eat within 6 months.

index

conversion charts

Weights and measures have been rounded up
or down slightly to make measuring easier.

Volume equivalents:

American	Metric	Imperial
1 teaspoon	5 ml	
1 tablespoon	15 ml	
¼ cup	60 ml	2 fl.oz.
⅓ cup	75 ml	2½ fl.oz.
½ cup	125 ml	4 fl.oz.
⅔ cup	150 ml	5 fl.oz. (¼ pint)
¾ cup	175 ml	6 fl.oz.
1 cup	250 ml	8 fl.oz.

Weight equivalents:

Imperial	Metric
1 oz.	25 g
2 oz.	50 g
3 oz.	75 g
4 oz.	125 g
5 oz.	150 g
6 oz.	175 g
7 oz.	200 g
8 oz. (½ lb.)	250 g
9 oz.	275 g
10 oz.	300 g
11 oz.	325 g
12 oz.	375 g
13 oz.	400 g
14 oz.	425 g
15 oz.	475 g
16 oz. (1 lb.)	500 g
2 lb.	1 kg

Measurements:

Inches	cm
¼ inch	5 mm
½ inch	1 cm
¾ inch	1.5 cm
1 inch	2.5 cm
2 inches	5 cm
3 inches	7 cm
4 inches	10 cm
5 inches	12 cm
6 inches	15 cm
7 inches	18 cm
8 inches	20 cm
9 inches	23 cm
10 inches	25 cm
11 inches	28 cm
12 inches	30 cm

Oven temperatures:

225°F	110°C	Gas ¼
250°F	120°C	Gas ½
275°F	140°C	Gas 1
300°F	150°C	Gas 2
325°F	160°C	Gas 3
350°F	180°C	Gas 4
375°F	190°C	Gas 5
400°F	200°C	Gas 6
425°F	220°C	Gas 7
450°F	230°C	Gas 8
475°F	240°C	Gas 9

FREE PUBLIC LIBRARY UNION, NEW JERSEY

3 9549 00422 6255